A GUIDE TO
SUCCOTH

by

RABBI ISAAC N. FABRICANT

B.A., H.C.F.

Minister, Brighton and Hove Synagogue

JEWISH CHRONICLE PUBLICATIONS
London

Published by
JEWISH CHRONICLE PUBLICATIONS
37 Furnival Street, London, EC4
© Isaac N. Fabricant, 1958

Made and printed in Great Britain by
THE SHARON PRESS
31 Furnival Street, London, EC4

A GUIDE TO SUCCOTH

CONTENTS

To my wife
HELENA
with love

INTRODUCTION

THE ORIGINS OF THE FESTIVAL OF SUCCOTH
THE SEASON OF OUR JOY

THE solemn strains and the haunting chants of entreaty
and praise which stir us from Kol Nidrei until the close
of Neilah are followed within a few days by the jubilant
chords of the liturgy of the Festival of our Joy. The
proximity of Yom Kippur and Succoth excites our
curiosity and invites speculation as to whether there
was some definite reason for coupling together these
two important Festivals, or whether it occurs by the
merest chance. The Midrash Rabbah, which expounds
by the use of homily rather than by a literal translation
or explanation, tells us in its whimsical manner that at
the termination of Yom Kippur God addresses Israel
with the words, 'Let bygones be bygones—from now
on we begin a new balance-sheet.' God uttered these
words because of the fasting and the supplication of
His people.

The Midrash continues that on the first day of
Succoth God addresses Israel, who stand before Him
lovingly holding the Lulab and the Ethrog, with similar
words of assurance. The message of the Midrash is that

the Festival of Atonement which is a Festival of Prayer cannot stand without the Festival of Succoth which is the Festival of Mitzvoth. It represents the synthesis of theory and practice in the pattern of Jewish belief.

The medieval Payyetanim[1] influenced by this Midrash composed a number of liturgical compositions to be recited on the Sabbath between Yom Kippur and Succoth. This Sabbath was regarded as the bridge between aspiration and fulfilment. The Hasidim[2] noted a common feature in the design of both Festivals, i.e. Yom Kippur and Succoth. On Yom Kippur the whole being of the individual is absorbed in prayer and meditation. Rabbi Bunam, a Hasidic leader who died in 1827, speaking of Succoth said: 'The command to dwell in a Succah during the Festival of Tabernacles is highly important, inasmuch as this is the only precept which we fulfil with our whole body.' Succoth follows close to Yom Kippur to stress the natural union between soul and body intended by our Torah for the service of God.

The critical point of view, however, will maintain

1 Writers of prayers mostly in poetical form for the *Machzor*, i.e. The Festival Prayer Book.

2 A religious movement which arose among the Polish Jews in the eighteenth century. The founder was The Baal Shem Tob or Besht as he was sometimes called (1700-1760).

that there is no connection between Yom Kippur and Succoth. Succoth was agricultural in origin, as can be seen from the name 'The Feast of Ingathering'. 'At the end of the year when thou gatherest in thy labours out of the field' (*Exodus* xxiii. 16, xxxiv. 22). 'After that thou hast gathered in from thy threshing-floor and from thy wine-press' (*Deut.* xvi. 13, 16).

Harvest Festivals were commonly observed by Canaanites. These, however, were characterised by obscene fertility rites and orgiastic scenes. In contrast, these Festivals were to be for the Israelites 'Holy Convocations' dedicated to the service of God and their fellow men.

The Festival of Succoth, which begins on Tishri 15 and lasts for eight (nowadays nine) days, is called זְמַן שִׂמְחָתֵנוּ, the Season of our Joy, in our liturgy. Every festival has its designation, but it is only the Festival of Tabernacles that is described as the 'Festival of our Joy'. The reason for this is as follows. There are three verses in the Torah enjoining the Israelite to rejoice during the Festival of Tabernacles. There is only one verse giving this injunction to rejoice in connection with the Festival of Shavuoth and no reference to joy whatsoever when the Bible refers to Passover. A commentator points out that since there was no in-

3

gathering of our fruits during Passover the Bible omitted the injunction to rejoice when speaking of this festival.

Judaism recognises the natural instinct of joy and makes no attempt to repress it, but rather to encourage natural self-expression. There are certain sects which affirm that the true worship of God can be achieved only through deprivation and rigid asceticism. These sects existed in the past and still have their adherents in our own time.

The Nazarite was commanded by the Scriptures to bring a sin-offering when the term of his Nazariteship had lapsed, and the reason given for this by Rabbi Eleazar Hakapar was that abstention from wine which the Nazarite vow involved was sinful. To draw away from a natural instinct of gladness with the fear that gladness might lead to vice is an admission of inability to exercise that restraint which requires strength of character. The Talmud declares: 'The Divine Presence does not abide in an atmosphere of gloom.' The Hasidim hold with Rabbi Eleazar Hakapar that a man whose life is replete with fastings and self-inflictions does not deserve the name of *Zaddik*;[3] and with the Jerusalem Talmud, that he who enjoyeth not what his eyes have seen will have

3 Righteous.

4

to answer for it on High; and, finally, with Samuel, that 'Whoever fasts is called a sinner.'

Once a Jew in great tribulation of heart came to the Besht[4], inquiring: 'How many days have I to fast, to make atonement for a grievous sin?' The Besht replied: 'Not through fasting is the ire of God averted, but through joy of which the Psalms are harbingers. Say the Psalms with inward rejoicing, and you will be quit of your sin.'

Men learned in the Law came to the Besht on an errand of dispute. 'In times gone by,' they protested, 'there were pious men in great numbers, fasting from Sabbath to Sabbath, and inflicting their own bodies with self-devised torments. And now your disciples proclaim it to all who care to listen that much fasting is unlawful and self-torment a crime.' The Besht answered: 'It is the aim and essence of my pilgrimage on earth to show my brethren by living demonstration how one may serve God with merriment and rejoicing. For he who is full of joy is full of love for men and all fellow-creatures.'

It was the genius of the teaching of our Torah which gave the inspiring message that joy as a human instinct is not proscribed, but it must not be allowed to run

4 The founder of Hasidism.

wild so that it degenerates into abandonment and licentiousness. In a reference to Shavuoth and Succoth, which were harvest festivals, the Bible enjoins: וְשָׂמַחְתָּ לִפְנֵי ה' אֱלֹהֶיךָ, 'And thou shalt rejoice before the Lord thy God.' The presence of God must be perceived in the midst of rejoicing over the material things of life. The awareness of the presence of God must be expressed by solicitude for those who need the help of their neighbours. (*Deut.* xvi. 14.) 'And thou shalt rejoice in thy feast, thou, thy son and thy daughter, and thy man-servant and thy maid-servant, and the Levite and the stranger, and the fatherless, and the widow, that are within thy gates.' Succoth thus became a vital commentary on the art of enjoyment. The Jew was taught through the Festival that real joy is a blending of the material and the spiritual.

Scholars have traced the origin of the injunction to dwell in booths, which has given the Festival the name of the Feast of Tabernacles, to the fact that in ancient times at the time of the olive and grape harvests it was usual to spend days and nights in booths. (cf. *Isaiah*. i.8. 'And the daughter of Zion is left as a booth in a vine-yard.') In *Leviticus* the Succah is given a symbolic meaning and is brought into relation with the wandering in the wilderness—'that your generations may

6

know that I made the children of Israel to dwell in
booths, when I brought them out of the land of Egypt.'
Thus the harvest festival is transformed into a historical
festival. The Kiddush recited on Sabbath and Festivals
stresses the need for the Jew to remember the event of
the departure from Egypt. The Succah was intended to
aid as a reminder of this historic event which declared
God to be not only the Creator but also the Lord of
History, who will through history in the course of
His own good time vindicate history as being not
merely the happenings of chance but a process culminating in the triumph of justice. Succoth is thus given a
place in the history of redemption and the Succah is a
symbol of protection for all times.

In *Leviticus* it is also prescribed that the Israelites on
the first day of the feast are to take to them the fruit of
goodly trees פְּרִי עֵץ הָדָר, branches of palm trees and
boughs of thick trees and willows of the brook, and
rejoice before God seven days.

The pious Jew derives great pleasure in selecting a
'goodly' Ethrog and he may even be excused his desire
to show his neighbours in synagogue the Ethrog which
has no 'flaws' and the box containing the fruit which
proclaims that it is for לִמְהַדְּרִין מִן הַמְּהַדְּרִין, 'for those
who glory in honouring the Mitzvah'.

CHAPTER I

THE SUCCAH:
ITS LAWS AND CUSTOMS

IT is a Mitzvah to begin building the Succah on the evening when Yom Kippur ends. The great Fast has not exhausted but rather refreshed the individual and in a mood of dedication he applies himself to the task of building 'the temporary residence'. The impermanence of the Succah is stressed emphatically in the Talmud, where it is ruled that the Succah must not be built higher than twenty cubits so as not to give it a permanent character. It is further enjoined that the Succah should not be lower in height than ten handbreadths as such a structure would not be fit as a residence.

In the season of plenty the Jew rejoices in his prosperity and in the rewards which his labours have brought him. He is inclined to delude himself into thinking that life is secure and durable. The Psalmist describes those people who are misled by their phantasy 'that trust in their wealth, and boast themselves in the multitude of their riches—their inward thought is that their houses shall continue for ever, and their dwelling places to all generations.' (*Ps.* xlix.) The Bible, however, through the law of the Succah brings man face to face with the realisation of the frailty of human life and the transience of human existence.

It is essential that the Succah is built in a manner which enables it to provide more shade than light. A Succah which does not allow this greater measure of shade is invalid—for the word Succah is derived from a verb which means 'to cover' and the logical corollary of covering is that it should produce shade. There is an interesting and significant regulation in the Shulchan Aruch which declares that even if the tent or hut is not made with the intention of fulfilling the Mitzvah of Succah, so long as it is built with the purpose of pro-viding 'shade' the Succah is ritually proper for the Festival.

Those who were perplexed by the hazards and the sorrows of Jewish history could draw confidence from the thought that the nations which basked in the glaring brilliance of applause and which thought that their successes were to be eternal were to be outlived by a people who would survive because of their reliance on God and because they dwelt within 'the shade of faith'. Isaac Arama (15th c.) in his work *Akedath Yitschak* dis-cussing this essential condition of 'shade' regards the

9

Succah as a vital symbol in Jewish ritual. It teaches that man must not have confidence in his own strength nor in his own fortunes but must place his faith in Divine Providence. For this reason the covering of the Succah of plants and leaves should not be laid on too thickly so that the heaven and the stars should be visible for 'the heavens declare the glory of God'. (*Ps. xix.*)

The medieval moralists found great scope for their religious teachings in the laws of the Succah. Rabbenu Bahya ben Asher (13-14th) speaks of the decision of Shammai to class as unfit an old Succah, i.e. a Succah that had been built earlier than thirty days before the Festival and without the intention that it would be used for the Festival that was to follow. This medieval moralist utilises the Succah to emphasise the profound lesson that symbols which have their roots in the ancient past must not be regarded as obsolete tradition but as observances which require renewal of interest and enthusiasm and even of language and terminology to engage the minds of each new generation.

Rabbi Joseph Caro, the celebrated author of the Shulchan Aruch of the sixteenth century, declared that the Succah provides a lesson on discipline. He argues that it would have been more appropriate that the Festival of Succoth should be observed in the month of Nisan since the Succah recalls the especial protection afforded by God to Israel when they left the land of bondage in Nisan. Nisan, however, is a month of intensely warm weather when people naturally leave their homes and retire to the booth in the field or garden where the shade can shelter them from the scorching heat of a relentless sun. Hence in Nisan the Succah would be ineffectual as a symbol. Tishri, the month of rains, was selected because whereas the rest of the world leaves the booth for the secure protection which the house offers, the Jew leaves the home and dwells in the Succah in order to show his readiness to fulfil the behest of his Creator.

It is worth noting that those customs which are inter-woven with home and family ceremonial have survived through the ages. The Seder, the Succah and other similar 'family' observances have captured the imagina-tion of our people and have strengthened home and family ties. In the days of Nehemiah when the leaders of Jewry realised the necessity of revitalising Jewish life they pressed this 'family' observance into service and soon the Succah made a dramatic appearance in garden, field, upon house roofs, in the house courts and in the broad places of the city gates.

To the mystic the Succah represented the ideal com-bination of physical and spiritual which is the mosaic of

Jewish thought. It is a place where one eats and drinks in an atmosphere of the joy of the Festival. It is also the place where one meditates and prays. R. Moses Cordovero, the sixteenth-century mystic of Safed, instituted a series of talks on the Torah, which he held in his Succah not only for his family but also for members of the Community. The Succah gave ample opportunity for אוּשְׁפִּיזִין, 'hospitality', and in the words of the Zohar: 'It is necessary for man to rejoice within the Succah and to show a cheerful countenance to guests. It is forbidden to harbour thoughts of gloom and how much more so feelings of anger within the portals of the Succah, the symbol of joy.'

The finest commentary on the Succah is the prayer which one recites on entering the Succah the first night of the Festival as an inauguration of the custom of dwelling in the Succah. 'May it be Thy will, O my God and God of my fathers, that Thou mayest cause Thy Divine Presence to dwell amongst us and mayest Thou spread the Tabernacle of Thy peace over us.' The Succah rewards those who inhabit it with a sense of deep and abiding tranquillity.

CHAPTER 2

THE FOUR PLANTS

THE 'Four Plants' which we are enjoined to bring during the Festival of Succoth are mentioned twice in our Scriptures. 'And ye shall take you on the first day the fruit of goodly trees, branches of palm trees and boughs of thick trees and willows of the brook, and ye shall rejoice before the Lord your God seven days.' (*Leviticus* xxiii. 40.)

The verse in Leviticus was the one which later generations accepted and translated into devoted practice. The Karaites were the only dissentients. In the time of the Maccabees already we hear that 'the people bore on the Feast of the Tabernacles branches and fair boughs and also palms and sang hymns in praise of God.' (2. *Macc.* x. 7.) Josephus in his work *The Antiquities of the Jews* stated that during the offering of the sacrifices in the Temple 'every one of the worshippers carried in his hands a branch of myrtle and willows joined to a bough of the palm tree, with the addition of a citron.' The Talmudical regulations which give detailed instructions as to how the plants should be held indicate that the custom of 'waving' the plants and of bearing them whilst in procession during the Service was widely in use before Mishnaic times.

When one delves deeper into the sacred words of our Scriptures the purpose of the bringing of the plants can be detected. The bringing of the plants and the 're-joicing before the Lord' was an implied protest against the nature-worship of the heathen. The primitive tribes worshipped nature because it was the source of their sustenance and prosperity. The Jew was to be exalted to a plane of concept and belief in consonance with his recognition of God as the Creator of Nature. The palm tree was and is to the Eastern mind the most perfect emblem of majesty, and the *ethrog* of beauty. To the Jew they were also symbols of the handiwork of God which 'recounts His glory'. The willows of the brook bring to mind the delightful banks of rivers and rills with all their freshness and coolness. The 'thick-leaved trees' are products of rich and luxuriant growth.

Some scholars maintain that at the harvest period the Jew was to bring the plants 'before the Lord' as an ex-pression of his gratitude for the bounty with which God has blessed humanity.

From early times there was a set formula for the 'waving' of the plants. They were waved in all directions during the recital of the Hallel—the exact order of the directions and the number of movements had to follow a fixed rule.[5] These are called נְעֲנוּעִים.

Our Rabbis regarded these 'wavings' as a vivid symbol of Israel's acceptance of the yoke of the Kingdom of Heaven. The Lulab pointing to the various directions proclaims to the world that the universe is the creation of God and that we His subjects must acknowledge His sovereignty by conformity to His laws. Others thought that the 'waving' which accompanies Israel's prayers were part of the supplication in which men plead that God should restrain 'evil winds' and 'evil dews' so that the climate upon which man's sustenance depends should be favourable (*Talmud Succah* 37). Some gave a mystical colour to their explanation when they declared that the pointing of the Lulab acted as an arrow to frustrate the designs of Satan.

Numerous are the homilies in Midrashic literature on the message of the four plants. The Midrash Tanchuma stresses a fundamental lesson on the word לָכֶם in the verse in *Leviticus* xxiii: 'And ye shall take unto yourselves the fruit.' God declares: 'I do not need the four plants but you, Israel, need them for your self-ennoblement.' The

5 Three movements upwards and three downwards towards the East, South, West and North.

four plants represent the combination of 'goodly' plants and those of lesser quality and these are brought into the service of God in unison. Similarly, it is essential that for the progress of society a strong bond of fellowship should unite all classes of men so that the influence of the righteous may have its effect on the minds and hearts of men of lesser character.

The Midrash stresses the vital lesson of the need for unity. These four plants possess sundry characteristics. Each plant differs from the other in some marked way. In the same way, men of differing characters must integrate themselves into society and exert to the full their usefulness. The Midrash continues and warns us that the return to the Holy Land will never be accomplished if Israel does not learn the lesson of unity.

Another passage in the Midrash reflects on the similarity of these plants to parts of the body. The Lulab resembles the spine of man, the myrtle branch the eyes, the willow the lips and the citron the heart. The bringing together of these plants teaches that we, too, must bring our faculties and dedicate them to the service of God. The Psalmist was inspired by the 'four plants' when he wrote: 'All my limbs shall say "O Lord, who is like unto Thee?" ' (Ps. xxxv. 10).

Through medieval literature until our own day many

writers have in accordance with their own interpretation given a philosophical or a mystical touch to this ancient injunction of the four plants. These plants bring to us not only the fragrance of vegetation but also that of thought to stimulate our interest in this ancient but perennial behest of our Creator.

CHAPTER 3

HOSHANAH RABBAH AND
SHEMINI ATZERETH

ON the first two days of Succoth and on each of the five days of Chol Hamoed 'Hoshanahs' are recited at the end of the Musaph Amidah. The Ark is opened, a Sepher Torah is taken to the Bimah and then follows the circuit of those carrying the four plants, whilst the Reader, who leads the procession, intones the appropriate Hoshanah for the day. These Hoshanahs have been composed in an arrangement of alphabetical order. This custom dates back to Temple times when a circuit was made around the Altar whilst proclaiming the words אָנָּא ה׳ הַצְלִיחָה נָא, אָנָּא ה׳ הוֹשִׁיעָה נָא, 'Save, we beseech thee, O Lord.' 'We beseech thee, O Lord, send prosperity.' Rabbi Judah used to say אֲנִי וָהוֹ הוֹשִׁיעָה נָא, 'O God, save we beseech thee.' (*Succah* 84.)

The fifth day of Chol Hamoed is known as Hoshanah Rabbah. In the Talmud it is described as 'Yoma Daravta', 'the day of the willow'. 'Hoshanah Rabbah' is a post-Talmudic designation.

In the Middle Ages the seventh day of Succoth became not only a day for the seven circuits with the Lulab and for the taking of seven scrolls to the Bimah, but it also assumed the rôle of 'Day of Judgment'. It became a sort of annexe to the Day of Atonement. The custom grew to spend the whole night preceding Hoshanah Rabbah in Biblical reading, including the Book of Psalms. This not only instructed but inspired deep meditation. When a visitor to Italy from Poland questioned this custom by quoting the *Tractrate Erubin* (p. 65), 'Night was created only for sleep', Samuel David Luzzatto (1800-1865) retorted with a passage from *Menachoth* (p. 110): 'Scholars who engage in study at night are performing a service as worthy as that of worship in the Temple.' 'And why should we not be awake during this night to pour out our supplications and meditations on the eve of the Seventh day of the Festival when momentous decisions of judgment come forth from the King as has been taught in the sacred work, the Zohar?'

In the folk-lore of the Middle Ages it was told how the Book on High in which was inscribed the destiny of the individual for the ensuing year was finally sealed on Hoshanah Rabbah. From the Middle Ages began the custom of white vestments for the Scrolls, the Desk and the Reader, which is a feature of Yom Kippur. In the Machzor Vitri[6], which is an important source for our knowledge of the liturgy of the Middle Ages, we note the custom of reciting in the Shacharith the series of Psalms which are added on Sabbaths and Festivals. From the fourteenth century onwards the custom arose in certain parts of the Orient and in those places where there was a special interest in mysticism to fast on Hoshanah Rabbah because it resembled Yom Kippur.

Towards the close of the Service it is the custom to strike a willow branch until the leaves fall off. In the days of the Temple they beat the dried twigs of the palm tree on the ground round the sides of the Altar. This was a signal for the children to loosen the Lulab and to remove the willow and the myrtle and then to eat the Ethrog.

The Rokeach[7] states that the willow plays a prominent part in the ritual of the Festival of Succoth because it is essentially a water-plant and its purpose is to remind us that we are being judged during the Festival as to whether we shall enjoy a plentiful supply of water or be deprived of this necessity of life. We supplicate with the words: 'Just as this willow grown by the banks of the river can only grow in the vicinity of water so mayest

6 A Machzor compiled by Simchah ben Samuel of Vitri, a pupil of Rashi (eleventh century).

7 A code compiled by Rabbi Eleazar of Worms (1160-1238).

Thou grant us water.' The popular explanation for the custom of the beating of the willow is that it symbolises the ephemeral aspect of life, for as the leaves of the willow drop through beating, so our years in which we are buffeted by the storm and stress of life fall from the span of time allotted to us. We must, therefore, make the fullest use of our years.

Shemini Atzereth, which is the eighth day of the Feast, is a Festival on its own and in the Kiddush recited in the evening we recite 'Shehechayonu'. The word עֲצֶרֶת is derived from a root which means 'to hold back' or 'keep in'. Since the seventh day of Passover is also designated as 'Atzereth' (*Deut.* xvi. 8) the word obviously conveys the meaning of 'closing festival'. Maimonides in his *Guide to the Perplexed* suggests that the eighth day was appointed in order to enable the people to complete those festivities for which the Succah would be inadequate and which require the normal surroundings of the larger home capable of holding a greater number of guests. Maimonides was undoubtedly influenced by the Targum כְּנִישְׁתָּא 'Assembly,' the rendering of the word 'Atzereth'. Rashi and others held 'Atzereth' to convey the idea of 'keeping or detaining in the Sanctuary another day' and of 'abstention from labour and worldly occupation'.

Josephus mentions that Shavuoth was known as 'Atzarta' and it was given this name because it was regarded as 'the closing feast of Passover'. The Midrash[8] introduces the thought of God's especial regard for the comfort of His people. Shemini Atzereth should similarly have been observed on the 'fiftieth' day after the first day of Succoth but because it would have been a strain for the people to make the journey to Jerusalem in the rainy season God fixed it as early as the eighth day.

It is the custom to eat in the Succah on Shemini Atzereth but not to recite the benediction over the command to sit therein (*Succah* 47a).

Shemini Atzereth is the occasion when we pray for rain. The Reader is dressed in white and various Synagogue appurtenances are suitably bedecked in white to mark the solemnity of the Service. In reality these prayers should be offered on the first day of Succoth[9] but rain falling on the Succah would cause

8 In the age of the Midrash 'Atzereth' was another name for Shavuoth. Because Shavuoth or Atzereth fell on the fiftieth day after Passover any other Festival described as 'Atzereth' should fall on the fiftieth day after the previous festival. Thus Shemini Atzereth should fall on the fiftieth day after Succoth.

9 The 15th of Tishri, the first day of Succoth, is, near enough, the period of the 'former' rain, and the handling of the four plants on the first day forms in Rabbinic thought a symbolic petition for rain.

inconvenience and hardship to those who love to dwell within the booth. Nevertheless, says one commentator, the four plants which grow near water are brought during the first day of the Festival and are a hint if not a direct reference to our dependence on water for our existence. Those of us who live in Western countries where there are no fixed seasons for rain are through the 'Geshem' prayers made conscious of the needs of the Holy Land which requires the rain in its due season as an urgent necessity. Thus Shemini Atzereth strengthens the ties between the Golah and the Yishub and brings us closer to the understanding of the essential teaching: 'All Israel are brethren'.

CHAPTER 4

SIMHATH TORAH

THE joy which permeates the Festival of Succoth, reaches its climax on Simhath Torah, the last day of the Festival. The festivities are centred around the ceremony of the circuits of the Sifrei Torah when hymns of prayer and praise are sung. A moving sight is that of the children carrying flags in procession, upon which are inscribed words speaking of the greatness of the Torah, and upon these flags is affixed an apple into which a candle is placed and kindled. Interspersed with these prayers and hymns which have found a place in the Machzor one hears, in many modern Synagogues, Israeli songs, and it is now a growing custom not to insist upon decorum and even to dance the Hora within the Synagogue itself.

The name Simhath Torah was not used until a relatively later date. It is not found as a name for the last day of the Festival in Talmudic literature. The custom of completing the Torah on the morrow of Shemini Atzereth originated in Babylon where they completed the reading of the Law in one year and spread to all Jewish centres by the end of the Gaonic period (about 1000 C.E.). The day was called 'the Day of the Book', 'the day of completion'. In time Simhath Torah became the commonly accepted name because the day was marked by joyous celebration. The name Simhath Torah is to be found in the Siddur of Rashi (11th c.). In the Middle Ages special vestments, adorned with ingenious skill by the women of the community, were put on the Sifrei Torah.

At first the celebration on Simhath Torah was held because of the joy that one had been privileged to be present at the completion of the reading of the Torah for the year. In the fourteenth century the reading of Genesis followed immediately upon the completion of Deuteronomy. The author of one of the great Codes of Jewish Law (R. Jacob ben Asher, 14th c.) Tur Orah Hayyim explained this custom thus—that Satan should not accuse Israel of wishing to end the Torah without the desire to begin again.

In the sixteenth century it became the custom to take out the Scrolls of the Law on the night of the twenty-second of Tishri, and to make circuits bearing the Scrolls around the Almemar. Various reasons are given for the seven circuits. Some say they correspond to Abraham, Isaac, Jacob, Moses, Aaron, Joseph and David; some to the seven Heavens, and others to the seven circuits around Jericho at the time of Joshua. There are some who maintain that they correspond to the Seven Sephiroth (spiritual forces emanating from God as expounded by the Kabbala, the teaching of the mystics).

In the morning many people were called to the Reading of the Law and certain verses in the closing chapters were read and re-read in order to give as many as possible the privilege of being called to the Torah. It was customary to call all the children towards the end of the Reading, and these all stood under a Tallith which was spread out over their heads in the form of a canopy. An adult who had been called with the children then recited the appropriate blessings and the children repeated these words slowly and solemnly after him. The verse *Genesis* xlviii. 16 was then recited. The blessing of Jacob for Ephraim and Menasseh was considered most suitable for the occasion. This custom prevails unto the present day.

The Torah has been given many names which express the love of our people for its Law. One of these names is כַּלָּה 'bride'. The celebration of Simhath Torah became a marriage feast and he who was called to the reading of the concluding verses of Deuteronomy was given the designation of 'Bridegroom of the Law'. At a later period the person who was called to the reading of

Genesis was called 'the Bridegroom of Bereshith'. In early times when these customs first began, the honour of being a bridegroom was given to distinguished scholars of the community. Later the practice was to offer it to the person who could donate most to the funds of the Congregation. Amongst the scholars who criticised this form of competition so that the privilege fell to the rich but unlearned was Immanuel of Rome (1270-1330 Italy).

In Jerusalem and in Oriental countries the bridegrooms were fêted as if they had been crowned. They sat on 'thrones' under canopies of silk and odes were sung in which the Law was extolled and the bridegrooms, too, received due honours in these compositions. So extravagant were the festivities in Italy, that in 1760 certain 'Takanoth' (communal edicts or measures for the benefit of the community) were instituted and excessive ostentation or lavish expenditure was restricted. In some communities the honour was given to those who had been married during the year. In Amsterdam the honour was not conferred by the wardens of the Congregation but democratically through a poll.

The Dubnow Maggid once explained to the Wilna Gaon the reason for the celebration of Simhath Torah being in Tishri and not in Sivan which is the anniversary of the granting of the Law. Why Simhath Torah at the conclusion of Succoth and not during Shavuoth? He states that Israel was compelled to receive the Torah during Shavuoth. All the nations of the world together with Israel declined to accept the Torah because of its impositions. God, however, knew that Israel alone had the potentialities to observe the Law and to become the teachers of the Law to the rest of the world. From Sivan to Tishri acquaintance with the Law ripened into love and with that love there grew a deep sense of joy. Whereas Sivan commemorates the acceptance of the Law, Tishri recalls the joy of the Law, and that joy has animated Israel in every generation.

CHAPTER 5

ECCLESIASTES: THE BOOK OF THE FESTIVAL

EARLY Midrashim already mention the custom of reading certain Scrolls during the Festivals. Ecclesiastes, which was selected for reading on the Sabbath Chol Hamoed of Succoth or Shemini Atzereth, was chosen because of the words, 'Divide a portion into seven, yea even into eight' (*Ecclesiastes* xl. 2), and therefore it was considered appropriate reading for the seventh and eighth days of the Festival.

This book was the subject of a heated debate by the Rabbis as to its worthiness to be included in the Canon. The view of the School of Hillel prevailed and it was finally accepted because of the summing up of 'Koheleth' the 'Preacher'. 'The end of the matter, all having been heard: fear God, and keep His Commandments; for this is the whole duty of man.' A modern writer, Menahem Rabulov, in an essay on '*Ecclesiastes* in the Festival of Succoth', emphasises the fact that neither *Proverbs* nor *Job* could take the place of *Ecclesiastes* and that the Bible would not be complete without this provocative work. *Proverbs*, he declares, is an 'objective' work on true wisdom representing the positive truths of Judaism whilst the arguments of a subjective Job, wrung from a heart saddened by chastening and from a mind in the turmoil of rebellion against a seemingly unjust judgment, are different from *Ecclesiastes* that stands between these two extreme attitudes.

Ecclesiastes is neither the passionate plea for faith nor the stormy disavowal of belief and resignation. It is a mixture of faith and denial, of hope and despair, of darkness and light, of joy and sadness and of life and death. *Ecclesiastes* was written by an author who desired to play the part of an instructor. He has his fellow-men before him, and feels that he has a lesson to convey to them. He is not a mere debater establishing opinions only to demolish them *ad absurdum*. Here is the practical philosophy of a man who realises that there are two sides or two contrasting facets of life—the existence of good and evil, the materialism and the spiritual grandeur of human life, the alternating moods of man himself— his inclination to follow the vanities and the follies for the pleasure they may bring and then the other mood of choosing the moral and the noble pursuits of life. We detect the swing of the pendulum in the writer himself. He is subject to these conflicting moods—the optimist and then the pessimist, the moralist and the *bon viveur*. The book reflects the constant friction between the two inclinations, the good and the bad in their battleground which is man himself. Although the mood varies, his verdict or judgment is stable. He attempts to inculcate a spirit of equanimity and to show that there is good even in things evil, and on the other hand the drawbacks incident to those things which men covet most.

The Festival of Succoth is surely the most appropriate period of the Calendar for the reading of this book which contains these contradictions. It is the Festival which occurs at a time of material abundance, and at the same time it is the Festival of deep spiritual experience. The Jew sees around him plenty and might imagine himself self-sufficient, when he is summoned to the Succah and peering through the scant covering above him, gazes at the heavens and contemplates his dependence upon God.

It was natural that Hillel should have defended this book. Hillel understood man's failings and realised that with all his shortcomings there was inherent good in every man. *Ecclesiastes* is the portrait of man who is perhaps the most inconsistent of God's creatures. Succoth is distinguished by its contrasting appeal and

Ecclesiastes was rightly selected as the manual which would proclaim this dual aspect of the Festival.

CHAPTER 6

THE STRUCTURE OF THE SERVICES OF THE SYNAGOGUE

FIRST AND SECOND DAYS

תְּפִלַּת עַרְבִית

Evening Service, p. 204 (*References are to Routledge Festival Prayer Book*).

The Piyyutim which intersperse the Evening Service and are known as the Maarabhoth because they are included in the Maaribh (Evening Service) were composed by Joseph ben Samuel Tobelem (Bonfils) of Limoges (11th c.) On page 205 there is a composition in which we ask God to grant Israel His protection because of the merit of the Patriarchs, Abraham, Isaac and Jacob. This is the doctrine of זְכוּת אָבוֹת, the Merit of the Fathers, which has played an important part in Jewish theology. When Israel is not worthy of the love and protection of God we implore that the righteousness of our ancestors should be credited to the account of their descendants.

The Maarabhoth of the Second Evening (pp. 215-218) were composed by Yechiel b. Isaac Michelmann of

Zülpich (13th c.). There is a long Piyyut on p. 216 written as an alphabetical acrostic and with the words repeated at the end of each verse 'on the Feast of Tabernacles'. Many of the customs connected with Temple worship which were observed during Succoth are mentioned.

תְּפִלַת שַׁחֲרִית

Morning Service.

The structure of these services is the same as that of the Sabbaths and the other pilgrimage festivals, viz., the introductory blessings and Psalms, the Shaharith (Morning Service), the Reading of the Law and the portion from the prophets (Haphtarah), and the Musaph. Full Hallel is recited.

Scriptural Readings: On both days the same portion of the Law is read and five people are called to the Reading, (*Leviticus* xxii. 24-xxiii. 14). If the festival falls on Sabbath seven are called. This Chapter contains the commandments relating to the observance of all the festivals. From the second Scroll on each day *Numbers* xxix. 12-16 is read. The sacrifices which were offered in the temple are enumerated.

The Haphtarah on the first day is read from *Zechariah* xiv because of the hope expressed by the prophets that all the nations of the world will one day assemble in Jerusalem to celebrate Succoth. On the second day the Haphtarah is from I *Kings* viii. 2-21. The celebration of the Consecration of the Temple which took place 'at the feast in the month Ethanim' is described. Ethanim was the name of the seventh month, which later became known as Tishri. The feast mentioned is Succoth. Solomon chose Succoth for this important ceremony because for the joyous occasion of the consecration he desired the atmosphere of joy which is the distinctive feature of Succoth.

הוֹשַׁעְנוֹת (page 143).

Hoshanoth.

The Ark is opened and a Scroll is taken to the Reader's desk and then a circuit is made with Ethrog and Lulab carried in the procession. The Hoshanoth throughout Succoth commence with the same entreaty, 'Save, we beseech Thee. For Thy sake, our God, save we beseech Thee.' God is called by four different names, 'Our God,' 'Our Creator,' 'Our Redeemer,' 'O Thou who seekest us.' In Hebrew these four names follow the alphabetical order. In the past there were versions in which God was described by names covering the whole of the alphabet, but these were considered too lengthy.

35

On the first day there follows a composition arranged in alphabetical order which is recited by the Reader during the circuit. This prayer was composed by Eleazar Kalir (9th c.), the greatest medieval writer of Piyyutim. In this prayer there is an appeal to God to save Israel for the sake of His attributes. On the second day the circuit is conducted during the recital of another composition by the same author, and in it there is the appeal that God saves the Holy City, Zion. With vivid language the author culls many descriptions of Zion and its sacred places from the Scriptures and Talmudic literature.

THE INTERMEDIATE DAYS

חוֹל הַמּוֹעֵר

Reference is made to the Festival in the daily Amidah because although the Festival is still celebrated work is permitted by those who are compelled to pursue their livelihood. The service is partly that of the ordinary weekday and partly that of the festival. Tefillin are removed before Hallel and the Ethrog and the Lulab are then taken for the recital of this prayer of praise. Unlike Passover only one Scroll is taken from the Ark for reading and portions are read each day from *Numbers* xxix which relate to the festival

sacrifices. Each day has its special composition for
Hoshanoth.

On the Sabbath of Hol Hamoed, Koheleth is recited
after Hallel. Two Scrolls are taken from the Ark and
from the first Scroll seven portions are read from
Exodus xxxiii. 12-xxxiv. 26. From the second is read a
portion from *Numbers* xxix. The Haphtarah is taken
from *Ezekiel* xxxviii. 18-xxxix. 16. After Musaph the
Ark is opened but no circuit is made since the Ethrog
and Lulab are not taken during the Sabbath. A composition by Eleazar Kalir is recited for Hoshanoth and in it
we implore God to save His people who keep the
Sabbath. The zeal and enthusiasm which the Sabbath
inspires is the theme of this richly worded prayer.

HOSHANAH RABBAH

הוֹשַׁעְנָא רַבָּה

There are additions to the Hol Hamoed Service
in the morning. *Ps.* 100 is recited as on all week-
days and *Ps.* 19 and the series of Psalms which are
recited on Sabbath and Festivals are added. *Ps.* 100
is recited because Hoshanah Rabbah is a week-day
and *Ps.* 19 and other Psalms are read because of the
singular importance of the day; it is a tradition that
Hoshanah Rabbah is the culmination of the Solemn-

Days commenced on Rosh Hashonah. Seven circuits are made. The first four circuits are made to the recital of Hoshanoth which were read during the previous days of Hol Hamoed. Then follow three Hoshanoth by Kalir, the third having many references to characters in the Bible and the appeal for the sake of the 'merit of the fathers' is reintroduced.

After the circuits prayers follow that make mention of the willow and water. The Lulab is laid aside and the bunch of willow is taken. Prayers for rain are offered and these are in a way an introduction to the special prayers for rain which are recited on the morrow, Shemini Atzereth.

SHEMINI ATZERETH

שְׁמִינִי עֲצֶרֶת

The maarabhoth of the evening were composed by Daniel ben Jacob (1200-1240) and contain repeated references to the departure from the Succah. Shehechayonu is said with the Kiddush because Shemini Atzereth is a 'Holy Day on its own'. In the morning two Scrolls are taken from the Ark. From the first *Deuteronomy* xiv. 22-xvi. 17 is read, and from the second *Numbers* xxix. 35-xxx. 1. The Deuteronomic reading concludes with the verse: 'Every man shall give as he is able, according to the blessing of the Lord thy God which He hath given thee,' and this has given rise to the custom of reciting the Yizkor, the memorial service for the departed, on each of the Festive days on which this portion is read. The giving of charity in accordance with one's means is considered the most fitting way to perpetuate the memory of our departed.

The Haphtarah is from I *Kings* viii. 54-66 which tells of Solomon and the ceremony of the Consecration of the Temple. 'On the eighth day he sent the people away, and they blessed the king; and they went unto their tents joyful and glad of heart.'

תְּפִלַת גֶּשֶׁם (page 138).

Prayer for Rain.

The Reader dons a white gown and the Scrolls of the Law read during the morning are similarly adorned with white vestments. The Ark is opened during these special prayers for rain. This prayer is sung solemnly by the Reader and the response is given by the Congregation. 'The merit of the fathers' is the central theme of this prayer. We implore that for the sake of our saintly ancestors God should send us water. One Rabbi, inspired at the thought of the Zachuth of the Fathers, exclaims: 'Blessed are Israel who can rely on the Zachuth of

Abraham and Isaac and Jacob, it is their Zachuth which saved them. It saved them on the occasion of the exodus from Egypt, when they worshipped the golden calf, and in the times of Elijah, and so in every generation.' (*Sifre*.)

SIMHATH TORAH

שִׂמְחַת תּוֹרָה

The absence of a reference to the 'joy of the Law' in the Maarabhoth is an indication that Simhath Torah, the Rejoicing of the Law, became the main feature of the Festival at a comparatively later period in the Middle Ages. After the Amidah a number of verses taken from different parts of the Bible are recited by the Reader and repeated by the congregation. These verses conclude with the customary prayers prior to the taking of the Scrolls out of the Ark. Seven circuits are made whilst a prayer composed in alphabetical order is recited and each verse ends with the words, 'Answer us on the day that we call.' In the morning the same introductory verses preceding the Opening of the Ark are recited, the circuits are made and the reading from three Scrolls then follows. From the first Scroll *Deuteronomy* xxxiii-xxxiv is read. Many people may be called to the Reading from this Scroll and it is the custom to call Cohen and Levi as the first two, and the three 'Israelim' follow and then again Cohen, Levi and three 'Israelim,' until the number to be called is completed. The last 'hamishi' (fifth portion) is reserved for the 'Kol Hanorim' (all the children) Aliyah.

The Reader then chants the passage beginning, 'With the permission. . . ' (page 191) [Authorship unknown] in which the Hathan Torah is called to the Law. The concluding verses of Deuteronomy are then read. The second Scroll then takes its place on the Desk and to it with a similar chant the Hathan Bereshith is called. *Gen.* i. 1-ii. 3 is read and portions of this first chapter are recited aloud by the congregation to signify the importance of the Creation in the thought of our people. From the third Scroll *Numbers* xxix. 35-xxx. 1 is read. The Haphtarah is read from *Joshua* 1. Moses died, but a successor was found to carry on his work.

After Ashrei a passage ascribed to Asher Halevi, of Worms, and commencing with the words, 'Blessed be he. . . ' (page 201), is chanted by the Reader in a joyful strain. It was composed by R. Amram, one of the Geonim (9th c.). It describes the death of Moses and concludes with the words, 'Moses died. Who shall not die? At the command of the Lord died Moses, our teacher.' Then follow two passages in which the Torah is extolled and the ascent of Moses to Heaven is described.

41

Other laudatory verses relating to the Torah are sung. The day is considered so joyful that the Cohanim are exempt from duchaning (Priestly benediction) because of the difficulty of concentrating on any duty other than that of the rejoicing of the Law.

CHAPTER 7

SUCCOTH THROUGH THE AGES

THE Book of Jubilees which was composed about 130 B.C.E. claims that Succoth was celebrated long before the granting of the Law. It declares that Abraham was the founder of the custom of the Festival of Succoth. When he came to live in Beersheba he set up his tents and instituted a ceremony which centred round these tents. He erected an Altar and made circuits around it accompanied by prayer—'And Abraham built Succoth for himself and his servants in the seventh month, and he was the first to celebrate the festival of Succoth in the Holy Land.' (*Book of Jubilees* 16. 26.) This book declares that this celebration which Abraham inaugurated was the inspiration for the law of Succoth found in our Torah.

There is an ancient legend based on *Genesis* xxxiii. 17, 'And Esau went to Seir—and Jacob came to Succoth.' In this legend Esau represents sin and temptation and Seir stands for the Day of Atonement. (*Leviticus* xvi. gives the law of Seir or goat on the Day of Atonement.) When Seir departed, i.e. the Day of Atonement, Jacob came to the Succah. Here is to be found the origin of the custom of beginning the building of the Succah soon after the termination of Kippur. There is a Midrash which tells us that Jacob not only observed Succoth but also added Shemini Atzereth.

In the days of the First Temple Succoth was considered the culminating Festival and because of its importance became known as הֶחָג, 'the Festival'. King Solomon chose this Festival as the occasion for the celebration of the dedication of the Temple. (1 *Kings*, Ch. viii, 2.)

Ezra and Nehemiah instructed those who had returned to Zion to build Succoth. Apart from the Mitzvah of the Succah which was taught in the Torah (they wished to establish the new State on the basis of the Torah) they were also anxious to recapture some of the splendour of former times, and Succoth with its rich ceremonial could provide the atmosphere they sought. The Bible tells us that those who returned co-operated with enthusiasm in the observance of the Festival and celebrated it so that the glory of former days returned.

In the days of the Second Temple the sacrifices were more lavish than at any other festival, requiring seventy animals. These sacrifices were made on behalf of the seventy heathen nations. The Rabbis declared: 'When the heathen destroyed the Temple, they destroyed the atonement that was made for them.' (*Succah* 55 b)

In addition to the colourful procession in the Temple in which the Lulab and the Ethrog were carried by the worshippers whilst the Hallel (*Psalms* 113-118) was recited there was the libation of water in the Temple on each of the seven days at the morning Service. According to the Mishnah a golden flask holding about three pints was filled with water from the fountain of Siloam, carried up to the Water Gate, where the procession was greeted by three calls on the ram's horn by the priests. The officiating priest ascended the ramp on the south side of the great Altar, and turned to the left (west), where there were two silver basins, one for the pouring of the wine, into the other the water was poured. At the moment when the priest was about to pour the water into the basin, the people shouted to him 'Raise your hand!' because once a certain priest spilled it on his feet. On one occasion Alexander Jannaeus (103-76 B.C.E.), king and high-priest, was pelted with citrons by the worshippers standing around because he showed contempt for the rite by spilling the water at his feet.

The pouring out of water had no Biblical support. According to R. Nehunya it was a law given by God to Moses at Sinai, but was not recorded in the Scriptures.

Scholars maintain that there was a belief current amongst many nations that the pouring out of water at the time when the first autumnal rains were due would magically induce rain to fall. Judaism would not tolerate this superstition and so it took an ancient custom of the nations and incorporated it in the Temple service, and the libation of water became a symbol of rain. The prayer for rain began to be recited in the Tefillah in the days of the Second Temple. R. Akiba explains the custom thus: 'Why does the Law say, Make a libation of water at the Feast? The Holy One, blessed is He, says Make a libation of water before me at the Feast in order that the rains of the year may be blessed to you.'

The Talmud gives a vivid description of the festivities on the termination of the first day of the festival. Tall candelabra were erected in the 'Court of the Women'. Every candelabrum bore four bowls, each holding seven and one half gallons of oil and cast off breeches and girdles of the priests were used as wicks. Young priests ascended ladders and poured their jars of oil into the basins. The light was so brilliant that it seemed more like day than night. Two galleries were built around three sides of the court for the spectators; in the upper one the women sat, in the lower the men. The separation of the sexes was felt to be necessary because of the 'levity' of the occasion. Men distinguished in the Community by their purity and character danced, with flaring torches in their hands, reciting appropriate verses in which God was praised. In the *Tractate Succah* we are told Rabban Simeon ben Gamaliel was so adept that, with eight torches going, not one of them touched the ground when he prostrated himself, touched his fingers to the pavement, bent down, kissed it, and at once sprang up (*Succah* 53 a).

There was an orchestra consisting of many instruments played by the Levites, who stood on the fifteen steps that led down from the court of Israel to the court of the women. These fifteen steps corresponded to the fifteen 'Songs of the steps', שִׁיר הַמַּעֲלוֹת, found in the *Book of Psalms* (120-134). There was a march through the court of the women, beginning at a signal on trumpets played by two priests, and moving to the sound of continuous trumpeting to the gate opening to the East. There they turned about facing west and said: 'Our fathers who were in this place stood with their backs to the Temple and their faces eastward, and worshipped the sun toward the east but our eyes are unto the Lord.' (*Ezekiel* viii. 16.) The joy at this ceremony was so great that the Talmud exclaims: 'A man who has never seen the rejoicing of the water-drawing has never

A GUIDE TO SUCCOTH

seen rejoicing in his life.' (*Succah* 53 b.)

In the Middle Ages the Succah brought the atmosphere
of the country-side to the squalid quarters of the ghetto.
The green leaves represented the fields and orchards of
the Holy Land for which they yearned and prayed. The
Rabbi delivered a discourse on the laws of Succoth some
time before the Festival and he appointed certain
learned individuals to tour the Jewish quarters between
Yom Kippur and Succoth in order to supervise the
making of the Succah. When a Jew could not afford
to build a Succah and to purchase the four plants he was
told to build the Succah in preference because of the
principle that 'that which is frequent precedes the less
frequent in priority'. The Succah is in frequent use like
the home, whilst the four plants are used only part of
the time.

In those dark days of the Middle Ages when it was not
easy to build the Succah, the bond of fellowship was
fostered by families uniting to share one Succah.

There were communities that could not obtain
foliage with which to cover the Succah. In those cases
they used straw and found some compensation for the
absence of more decorative covering in the thought
that the letters of קַשׁ, the Hebrew word for 'straw',
could stand for the initial letters of קְרַע שָׂטָן, 'destroy

48

Satan'. They could be forgiven the thought that their calumniators who were all around them, were the Satan to which they referred.

The medieval Succah was bedecked with the fruits which the Bible mentions grow in the Holy Land. The Holy Land was brought to the Succah. John Buxtorf (17th c.), a Christian Hebraist, recorded the fact that he saw a Succah which was decorated with eggs upon which were inscribed verses relating to Succoth. He wondered as to what was the origin of the custom. In some communities it was the custom to kindle a light each night of the Festival, in honour of the אוּשְׁפִּיז (one of our heavenly guests or spirits of our ancestors) for that day and in other communities seven lights each night for the seven heavenly guests.

In the Middle Ages it was often difficult to acquire an Ethrog to comply with all the requirements. It was to be a 'goodly' fruit. The distance from the countries which grew the Ethrog to the ghetto areas of Europe was considerable, and travelling was not easy. Yet men went on long journeys to obtain the fruit. The story is told that the community of Wilna were anxious to acquire an Ethrog which should be worthy of the Wilna Gaon (1720-1797), the most renowned Talmudical scholar of that age. A representative was sent but he found great difficulty because it was a year of drought. Eventually he arrived at an inn, and to his intense joy he saw an Ethrog which was 'goodly' in every respect. 'Would you sell me your Ethrog?' asked the messenger of Wilna. 'I do not trade in Ethrogim. This is mine and it will be for my use during the Festival,' replied the innkeeper. 'I want to purchase the Ethrog on behalf of the Wilna Gaon,' said the messenger. The innkeeper was deeply moved at the mention of the name of the famous sage. 'He will receive it from me as a present,' he said. He continued, 'However it will be given on one condition, namely, that the Mitzvah which the Gaon will fulfil must be in my name. The Mitzvah must be credited to me.' The messenger was not pleased with the transaction but nevertheless accepted the Ethrog on those terms. When the Gaon heard of the condition he was overjoyed. He said 'I am now privileged to fulfil a Mitzvah without an ulterior motive. This is a Mitzvah which will not bring me a reward.'

In some communities it has been the custom to distribute charity throughout the town so that the poor might not find the task of building a Succah and adorning it beyond their means. A Hasid Rabbi known as the Tzanzer (d. 1876) when asked why he insisted upon special charity for Succoth replied, 'We are commanded to adorn the Succah. And what better ornament can there be than the distribution of charity among those who lack the means wherewith to be glad in the "season of rejoicing"? '

In modern times in Western countries, the Succah has become an important adjunct to the Synagogue. The Synagogue Succah draws large congregations for Kiddush after service and it has become a centre for the gathering of people congenial because of its pleasant surroundings and distinctive atmosphere. The Succah of the home is making way for the Communal Succah. This appears to be a modern trend which is spreading far and wide.

CHAPTER 8

THE TRANSIENCE AND PERMANENCE OF HUMAN LIFE

DURING the Festival of Succoth our thoughts turn not only to the Succah 'the temporary residence' but to life itself which is of short duration. Meditation as to the fleeting nature of life can lead to one of two possible results. It can be argued that if life is so insecure and is so much like 'a dream that flieth away' it is of little value and all available time should be spent in reckless living and with the object of seizing every ounce of 'pleasure' out of life. There was one school of thought founded by Epicurus, the Greek philosopher, which encouraged its followers 'to eat, drink and make merry for tomorrow we die'.

The *Book of Proverbs* has as its mission the teaching of 'wisdom'. It is wise to understand life. Is life merely physical and its end death or is its essence spiritual and will issue forth into eternity? The school of pessimistic thought could only see the downward trend of life. It could only behold the vigour of man deteriorating with age until feebleness ended with the grave. The *Book of*

Proverbs held the view that life need not decline but it could ascend to great heights. 'The path of life goeth upward for the wise that he may depart from the netherworld beneath.' (*Proverbs* xv. 24.) The *Book of Ecclesiastes* which is read during Succoth tells us of man's physical descent. It speaks of the last years of man's life: 'Before the evil days come and the years draw nigh when thou shalt say: "I have no pleasure in them." ' (xii. 1.) The writer maintains that life is transient but it is also permanent because the spirit returns to God and thus survives. 'And the dust returneth to the earth as it was, and the spirit returneth unto God who gave it.' The Psalmist stressed the fact that the shortness of life is inevitable and that wealth cannot stay the oncoming of death. Why should men be filled with arrogant pride when they have acquired vast possessions? Their mastery over the material things of life is only of short duration (*Psalm* 49). Thus the Psalmist endeavoured to teach that the knowledge of the transience of life must induce the right conduct in life. Wealth is as ephemeral as life itself but 'righteousness endureth forever'.

In Rabbinic thought man stands between the angels and the beasts of the earth. His life is transient since he is unlike the angels who live forever, but he can merit eternal life in the world to come and this distinguishes him from brute creation which has existence only in this world. 'God said, "If I were to create him entirely according to the nature of the angels, he would live forever, and never die; if I were to create him entirely according to the nature of the animals, he would die, and not live again; so behold I will create him with something of the natures of both; if he sins, he shall die, if he does not sin, he shall live." ' (*Genesis Rabbah* viii. ii.)

Even more explicit is the statement of Rabbi Simlai (latter part of the second century): 'All the creatures that were created from the heaven, their soul and their body was from heaven (of celestial substance); and all the creatures that were created from the earth, their soul and their body was of the earth, except man, whose soul is from heaven, his body from the earth. Therefore if a man keeps the law and does the will of his Father who is in heaven, he is like the creatures above, as it is written, "I said ye are divine beings, and sons of the Most High, all of you"; but if he does not keep the law and do the will of his Father who is in heaven, he is like the creatures below, as it is written, "Surely like man ye shall die." ' (*Psalm* lxxxii. 6-7.)

Man is mortal but his spiritual being is immortal. He is greater than the angels who are not tempted to sin. Man's greatness lies in his capacity to war with the evil inclination which lies in wait within him. The victory of the 'good' over the 'bad' invests man with unique distinction amongst the subjects of God. R. Joshua b. Levi said: 'When mortal man goes on his road, a troop of angels proceed in front of him and proclaim: "Make way for the image of the Holy One, blessed be He."' (*Deut. Rabbah.*)

The medieval Jewish philosophers and moralists found the mortality and immortality of man a fascinating theme. Maimonides (1135-1204) held the optimistic view that the world is not the passage between birth and death, between the cradle and the grave, but rather it is the training ground for man's spiritual development. In his Commentary on the Mishnah on Abot iv. he writes, 'After death there is no opportunity for man to attain perfection or increase of virtue; he can only do so in this world. Solomon hints at this when he says, "There is no work, nor device, nor knowledge, nor wisdom in the grave whither thou goest" (*Ecclesiastes* ix. 10); but these objects, which a man should pursue, remain for him so long as he lives. Therefore it is obligatory that he should strive for them during his brief span of life and not waste his time in the acquisition of anything but the virtues; because his loss is great if he neglects his opportunities, since he can never repair it.'

In Jewish teaching, man himself is the arbiter of his own life; he can make it transient or permanent. Significant in this connection is the answer commonly given to the question: 'Why after the creation of man are there not written the words, as in the case of cattle, "And God saw that it was good"?' (*Genesis* i. 25.) All other creatures, the answer runs, received their final nature at the time of creation. But man was endowed with the faculty of free-will or self-improvement. Hence it was impossible to declare concerning him that he was good at the time of his creation. It was fitting to discover first what he would make of himself.

Moses Hayyim Luzzatto (1707-1747) in his work *Mesillath Yesharim* declares that man's circumstances, whether fortunate or unfortunate, are a source of trial. So poverty and so wealth. 'Lest I be full and deny, and say, "Who is the Lord?" or lest I be poor and steal, and profane the name of my God (*Proverbs* xxx. 9).' If he is valorous and conquers his enemies (his temptations), he becomes the perfect man who earns the privilege of communing with his Creator. Then he will pass from the vestibule of this world into the palace to enjoy the Light of Life. To the extent that a man subdues his evil inclinations, keeps aloof from the things that prevent him from attaining the good, and endeavours to commune with God, to that extent is he certain to achieve the true life and to rejoice in it.

We cannot measure life quantitatively. It is not the number of years but rather the quality that determines whether life is transient or permanent. The Rabbis had this thought in mind when they said, 'In one brief hour a man can achieve eternity.' Succoth is the season of plenty. Material prosperity is a challenge to man to use wisely his means and to live the spiritual life. Succoth is intended to remind the Jew of the transience of the physical and the material, but it also stresses the opportunities we have, in our handling of the physical, to reach the heights and to attain a permanence of life.

CHAPTER 9

PARTICULARISM AND UNIVER-SALISM IN JEWISH THOUGHT

THE teaching that the Jews were selected in the first years of Israel's nationhood as 'the people of God' with a particular mission has given rise to misconceptions and distorted opinions. In recent years propagandists who were defending their racial theories, which held that certain types of nations were superior, pointed to the early chapters of Exodus which speak of the selection of Israel as the source for such theories. For them, the Bible confirms the theory of selectiveness.

In *Exodus* xix. there are two verses which proclaim Israel as the peculiar treasure of God and declare that this distinctiveness will be earned if Israel keeps the covenant of God. 'Now, therefore, if you will obey my voice indeed, and keep My covenant, then you shall be a peculiar treasure to Me above all nations: for all the earth is Mine. And you shall be to Me a kingdom of priests and a holy nation.' The words 'for all the earth is mine' refutes the fallacy that in the Pentateuch God is but a national deity. He is God of all the earth and He has chosen Israel for a special task. The Israelites should be among the other nations what the priests are in one nation; they were selected to teach and spread the doctrine of God, and thus to become the teachers and prophets of the nations. Kalisch in his *Commentary on Exodus* writes, 'The priests form, in many respects, the medium between God and the people; and thus it was the grand vocation of Israel to be the medium between the nations of the earth and God, to bring all the nations to God, and thus ultimately to form one whole with the rest of the world, to cease to be a chosen people, because they had made the truth of God a common property of mankind.'

The selection of Israel did not confer upon them any material benefits. They were not automatically favoured with wealth and security. As a people they have suffered more than any other nation because of the doctrine of God, which they would not reject even on pain of death. The title of 'teacher' implied certain responsibilities and when they neglected the teachings which they were appointed to impart to the world they were punished all the more. The sin of the teacher is more grave than that of the pupil. 'Hear this word that the Lord hath spoken against you, O children of Israel, against the whole family which I brought up out of the land of

Egypt, saying: You only have I known of all the families of the earth; therefore I will visit upon you all your iniquities.' (*Amos* iii. 2.)

'Isaiah lii. 13-liii speaks of Israel as being not only the prophet of the true religion but its martyr, its witness in suffering; as the teacher of the world Israel bears the penalty which others have deserved, and when its day of vindication comes and God greatly exalts it, the nations which despised it in the time of its humiliation will confess in amazement that through its sufferings they were saved.' (George Foot Moore in his work *Judaism*.)

In Rabbinic literature there are many passages which reflect the particularist attitude of the sages. R. Yudan said: 'The world was created for the sake of the Torah.' R. Joshua b. Nehemiah said: 'For the sake of the tribes of Israel' (*Genesis Rabbah*). This particularist outlook was not one of conceit or arrogance. Choice of Israel implied certain responsibilities and Israel was charged to care for others because of its specialised knowledge and inherent capabilities. God says, 'Of all the peoples I have created I love only Israel,' as it is said, 'Because Israel was young, I loved him' (*Hos.* xi. 1.), and 'Of all the things that I have created, I love only justice,' as it is said, 'I, the Lord, love justice' (*Is.* lxi. 8) 'so I will give

the thing which I love to the people whom I love'
(*Deut. Rabbah*).

The Jews were like all nations particularistic. But
other nations were interested only in their particular
destiny and if their ambitions were opposed they
ruthlessly challenged the nation standing in their way.
There was no regard for the destiny of the other nation.
Even Plato in his 'Republic' outlined his universal
state as being one in which Greeks are arrayed against
non-Greeks in constant warfare; war being one of the
necessary evils. Professor Lazarus in his *Ethics of Judaism*
writes, 'It was part of Jewish particularism that the soul
of the people was filled with the universal ideal, with
the promise, the hope, the requirement that mankind
be a unit in its highest goal. Ethically this was the point
of sharpest contrast between Jews and their neighbours,
the radical, distinctive quality which constituted their
superiority over the others. To cultivate this quality, to
make it effective, Israel had to segregate itself. In a word,
Israel had to be particularistic in order to formulate and
hold up the universal ideal.'

The Jews were only made a particular nation so that
the Revelation should be proclaimed to all the nations
of the world. Israel's exclusive possession of the teaching
of God was not the end, but the means to a greater end.

The providential care of God for all mankind and the future recognition of the true God by all nations are common themes in the Psalms. The selection of the *Book of Jonah* for public reading on Yom Kippur showed the universalistic attitude of the Rabbis. We as a people solicit God's pardon not only for our sins but also for the transgressions of the other nations of the world. Jonah, who had a narrow particularistic attitude, was proved wrong. He was taught that the view of the Jew must not be narrow but broad, embracing the welfare of the world and not just one section of it. Succoth continues with this vital teaching. The Haphtarah for the first day of Succoth is from *Zechariah* xiv. 'And it shall come to pass, that every one that is left of all the nations that came against Jerusalem shall go up from year to year to worship the King, the Lord of Hosts, and to keep the feast of tabernacles.' (v. 16.) The Tabernacle will be wide enough to admit the world which will acknowledge God as King over all the earth; 'In that day shall the Lord be One, and His name one.' (v. 9.) The offerings during the Festival of Tabernacles represented the seventy great peoples and the sacrifices were intended to atone for these nations. From a number of passages in the Talmud and Midrash it is evident that the Sages thought that there were seventy great nations and seventy tongues in the world of their day. Israel will not be deterred from the task of praying and caring for the nations of the world. We recall the words of the Psalmist, 'In return for my love they are become my adversaries, but I pray.' (*Ps.* cix. 4.) It has also been suggested that the waving of the Lulab in all directions represents our concern for peoples in all parts of the globe. The Lulab is the symbol of the universalism of Judaism.

Can we not explain why Zechariah had the vision of all the nations of the world going on pilgrimage to Jerusalem during the Festival of Succoth? Why did he single out the Festival of Tabernacles in his picture of a united world bound by the closest ties of fellowship? Tabernacles is the Festival of material prosperity. The cause of strife between the nations of the world is greed and the envy of one nation for another's possessions. Economic causes are generally at the basis of the problem of conflict. The prophet dreamed that these economic factors would recede from the world scene and during the Festival of material plenty the nations would show that they could share the resources of the world equitably and live in peace in the world which would become סֻכַּת שָׁלוֹם, 'the tabernacle of peace'.

CHAPTER 10

THE PLACE OF JOY IN HUMAN LIFE

THE Festival of Tabernacles, which is known as the 'Festival of our Joy,' is also the period for meditation and introspection. *Ecclesiastes*, which is read during the Festival, at times evokes the sombre atmosphere of the house of mourning where one can contemplate the shortness of life and its purpose. At other times the author invites his readers to lose themselves in jollity. The reader of *Ecclesiastes* is left with the impression when he has completed the book that Judaism counsels one to follow a middle path between the two extremes of hilarity and weeping. He should pursue a moderate joy.

W. B. Yeats in one of his poems writes, 'But joy is wisdom.' If joy is wisdom, it is therefore wise to cultivate it as a virtue for it is no casual emotion. One can train oneself to be joyful. Joy wisely experienced invests life with that quality of happiness which is necessary for a full existence. Without joy human life becomes bleak and full of despair.

No true worship of God can be achieved without joy.

The Psalmist exhorts the worshipper to serve God with joy because this is the only manner in which one can adequately pay homage to God. 'Serve the Lord with gladness: come before his presence with exultation.' (*Ps.* c. 2.) 'Let the righteous be glad; let them exult before God; yea, let them rejoice with gladness' (*Ps.* lxviii. 3.), 'Let Israel rejoice in His Master; let the children of Zion be joyful in their King.' (*Ps.* cxlix. 2.)

Solomon declared that the nearer we approach God in thought and deed the deeper will be our joy. Religion should not make a person afraid. If a person fulfils religious precepts through fear of the consequences of omission, he approaches God negatively. Knowledge of God's will and a proper understanding of His teachings, will bring man nearer to God through love and this sense of nearness will bring joy to the heart of the worshipper. 'Draw me to Thee, we will run after Thee; the King hath brought me into His chambers; we will be glad and rejoice in Thee.' (*Canticles* i. 4.)

In *Deuteronomy* there are recited the grave punishments which will follow sin and wrongdoing. Sin will bring tragedy in its wake. One of the sins mentioned is the worship of God as an onerous and disagreeable task. 'Because thou didst not serve the Lord thy God with joyfulness, and with gladness of heart.' (*Deuteronomy* xxviii. 47.)

The Rabbis declare that commandments do not tire or exhaust the joyful worshipper. He always yearns for more and more commandments, as the fulfilment of each is a joy to him (*Deuteronomy Rabbah*). The Rabbis interpreted *Ecclesiastes* ii. 2, 'I said of laughter, it is to be praised.' That is, the joy of the commandment (*Sabbath* 30.b.). 'The Holy Spirit does not rest where there is idleness, or sadness, or ribaldry, or frivolity, or empty speech, but only where there is joy' (*Midrash Psalms*).

In the world to come a man will be rewarded for the joy he felt in the observance of the Mitzvah rather than for the fulfilment of the Mitzvah itself. The Rabbis hear God saying to the person concerned about his lot in the world to come, 'If you have fulfilled My words with joy, My servants will come to greet you, and I Myself will go forth to meet you, and say to you, "May your coming be in peace."'

Many of the passages of the Talmud extolling the joy of the Law date from the time when the Jews were being denounced because they adhered to a Law which was described by the critics as a law of harsh slavery. A passage in the Talmud gives a picture of the zeal and joy with which the Jew observed his commandments. According to *Deuteronomy* xxiv. 19, a sheaf forgotten in the harvest field belonged to the poor; the proprietor being forbidden to go again and fetch it. One could only observe this precept by forgetfulness. 'It happened to a Hasid that he forgot a sheaf in his field, and was thus enabled to observe the commandment with regard to forgetfulness. Whereupon he instructed his son to go to the Temple, and offer for him a burnt-offering and a peace-offering, whilst he also gave a great banquet to his friends in honour of the event. Thereupon his son said to him, "Father, why dost thou rejoice in this commandment more than in any other law prescribed in the Torah? He answered, that it was the occurrence of the rare opportunity of accomplishing the will of God, even as the result of some oversight, which caused him so much delight." '

There are many references to joy in worship in the devotional literature of the Middle Ages. Bachya ibn Pakuda, the author of *Duties of the Heart* (1040-1110), maintains that the joy experienced in the performance of the Mitzvah is the reward for the Mitzvah. R. Joseph Askari of Safed (16th c.) makes joy one of the necessary conditions without which a law cannot be perfectly carried out.

In Hassidic literature much has been written on the place of joy in the worship of God. The Mezeritzer

Maggid (d. 1772) said, 'When a king is at a celebration he is approachable to many people who otherwise would be denied admittance to the palace. Likewise when we serve God with joy, He is more approachable.' 'Weeping is evil indeed, for man should serve God with joy. But if one weeps from joy, tears are commendable.'

Not only in our relationship with God but also in our association with our fellow-men Judaism counsels us to adopt a cheerful attitude and to greet our neighbours with a happy disposition. In the *Ethics of the Fathers* (1. 15) Shammai advised, 'Receive all men with a cheerful countenance.' It is interesting to note that Shammai was himself inclined to be short-tempered and morose, and in this statement can be detected the realisation of his own shortcoming, and the inner struggle to conquer his weakness.

One of the great merits of the Hasid is that he will not allow sorrow to oust the joy in his heart. The Alexanderer Rabbi (d. 1870) said, 'We read in Isaiah lv. 12, "For ye shall go out with joy." This means, "If we are habitually joyful, we shall be released from every tribulation." ' No life is free from anxiety and sorrow, but the cultivation of joy and happiness as a philosophy of life can dispel the gloom which invades the soul of man in the hour of grief. This joy of living encourages the mood of optimism, and with joy accompanying us in all our experiences there is interwoven faith in the rule of God.

When Rabbi Elimelech of Lizensk (d. 1810) perceived that his end was approaching he became very cheerful. There was intense joy in all that he spoke to his disciples. One of his disciples inquired the reason for his unusual mood. The Rabbi thereupon took the hand of his faithful disciple into his own, and said, 'Why should I not rejoice, seeing that I am about to leave this world below, and enter into the higher worlds of eternity? Do you not recall the words of the Psalmist, "Yea, though I walk through the valley of the shadow of death, I will fear no evil, for Thou art with me." Thus does the grace of God display itself.'

Every Festival in the Calendar of our people makes its contribution towards the philosophy of our people through its distinctive teaching. The Festival of Succoth, which is the 'Festival of our Joy,' inspires joy not only during the days of its celebration but teaches that joy is a fundamental attitude in Jewish life and joy is the companion of faith which has preserved the soul of our people through our long and illustrious history.